Women Should Never...

Women Should Never...

(A How-NOT-to Guide for the Modern Woman)

by Clare Woodcock and Helena Owen

**Andrews McMeel
Publishing**

Kansas City

05 06 07 08 09 BID 10 9 8 7 6 5 4 3 2 1

ISBN: 0-7407-5046-1

Library of Congress Control Number: 2004111632

Women Should Never...

. . . sit in the back of the car
while their husbands are driving.

. . . wear crushed velour
track suits.

. . . collect porcelain dolls.

. . . commission large, misty, sexy studio photographs of themselves.

. . . wear saucy, off-the-shoulder milkmaid blouses.

. . . wear stirrup leggings.

. . . possess unbranded
pink and white tennis shoes.

... expose gnarled, discolored
toenails in sandals.

. . . wear the same clothes
as their mothers for trips
out together.

. . . crave their mothers'
hairstyles.

. . . declare that
the Dress Barn
is their favorite shop.

. . . have mustaches.

. . . have tobacco-
stained fingers.

. . . wear slips that are
longer than their skirts.

. . . allow eyeliner
to clog their tear ducts.

. . . wear plastic
clip-on earrings.

. . . wear miniskirts if they
have fat legs.

. . . reveal cracked,
hard skin in sling-back
sandals.

. . . wear skull rings.

. . . ask if they can inspect
their boyfriends' boils.

. . . pop their boy-
friends' pimples.

. . . refer to their pet cats
as "the girls."

. . . wear knee socks
over stockings.

... have hickeys.

. . . carry clutch bags.

. . . wear diamond-
studded denim.

. . . wear earrings made
from feathers.

. . . dress babies in suits.

. . . wear pocket watches.

. . . have side ponytails.

... wear slippers to stores.

. . . call their husbands
"my fella."

. . . buy underwear from
Frederick's of Hollywood.

. . . like underwear from
Frederick's of Hollywood.

. . . go by the name Bitsy.

. . . assume baby
voices are sexy.

. . . wear stiletto heels
with jeans.

. . . wear football team T-shirts.

. . . make their boyfriends
wear the other half.

. . . miss evenings out
with friends in case
their boyfriends call.

... wear any kind of
belted dress.

. . . shave their faces.

. . . wear their keys on a chain
hanging from their belt loop.

... tuck in their sweaters.

. . . propose to their boyfriends
on national television.

. . . wear cartoon character
socks with knee-length skirts.

... wear jeans with
elastic waistbands.

. . . wear legwarmers under
the illusion that they
are still in style.

. . . wear white sports socks
with dress boots.

. . . tuck their jeans
into their boots.

. . . wear black, opaque hose
with white shoes.

. . . call their husband "Dad."

. . . stick their tongues out when
they concentrate.

. . . carry small dogs in
shopping bags.

. . . have lipstick on their teeth.

. . . spit.

. . . pay for every date.

. . . wear golf sweaters.

. . . wear broken-heart
necklaces.

... insist their husbands wear
homemade sweaters.

. . . wear sheer hose
if they haven't
shaved their legs.

... collect thimbles and
have a cabinet for them.

. . . knit sweaters
for their dogs.

. . . aspire to achieve
Madonna's '80s look.

... become a punk if they
are over sixty.

. . . call their husbands
"my better half."

. . . buy lingerie from Avon.

. . . pack their boyfriends'
bags for overnight trips.

. . . be impressed by a
meal at Red Lobster.

. . . ask a man if he's received
her Valentine's card.

. . . put love notes in their husbands' lunches.

. . . wear gold necklaces
that have their names
written in script.

. . . think it's a man's right to
have his dinner on the table
at five-thirty every day.

. . . perm their bangs.

. . . like shoes with kitten heels.

. . . insist their fiancés wear vests to match the bridesmaids' floral dresses.

. . . have Dolly Parton hair.

. . . wear heavily laced,
ill-fitting bras under blouses.

. . . jog without a sports bra.

. . . iron their husbands'
tighty whities.

. . . drink mugs of Guinness.

. . . simply invent names for
their children, like Caprina
or Belvedere.

. . . buy clothes in a dress size
smaller than they really are.

. . . wear blue mascara.

... wear sweaters with cute
kitten prints on them.

. . . buy chandeliers for
small houses.

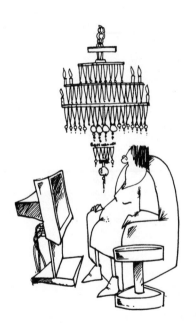

. . . wear crocheted hats.

. . . shout abuse at the ref when
attending a football game.

. . . tie ribbons in their
dogs' hair.

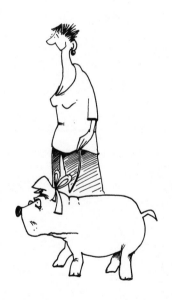

. . . wear black bras under white tops.

. . . put their makeup on when
driving down the highway.

. . . feed their boyfriends
in public.

. . . name their children after
soap stars.

. . . listen to their mothers' ideas
of a suitable boyfriend.

... wear cute night-shirts.

. . . refer to their husbands by pet names in public.

. . . count calories during every
meal and snack.

. . . wear thong leotards.

. . . have a "Love is . . ."
bedspread.

. . . dress as wenches to take part in
medieval battle reenactments.

. . . give their boyfriends
piggyback rides.

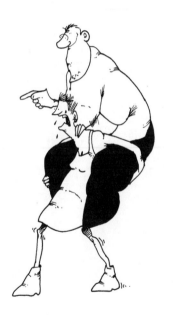

. . . knit sweaters for
their favorite TV celebrities.

. . . play the trombone.

. . . talk about men's "packages."

. . . talk about their
gynecological history in
a post office line.

... be happy when their man
orders for them in a restaurant.

. . . work with their husbands
in a children's traveling
theater company.

. . . admire the career
of RuPaul.

... have a crush on
Carrot Top.

. . . carry screwdrivers
behind their ears.

. . . have fistfights.

. . . say "my husband
likes you."

. . . keep a flip-chart at home to
illustrate things to their families.

. . . use a laser pointer.

. . . hang lacy curtains
over garden shed windows.

. . . sniff a baby's bottom
to check if the diaper
needs changing.

. . . admit to burping
on the first date.

. . . give public demonstrations
on spinning
raw sheep's wool.

... talk wistfully about
weddings on a first date.